**BATTLESHIPS
1897-1945**
R. A. Burt

Front cover illustration:
The 'pocket battleship'
Deutschland in 1935; see plate
66.

Back cover illustrations:
Top: The battlecruiser *Moltke*
on trials; see plate 31.

Bottom: The battleship
Westfalen, 1909-10; see plate
21.

1. *Kaiser Friedrich III*. When
Kaiser Wilhelm II came to the
throne he brought with him the
desire for an adequate fleet
which would protect Germany's
coastline in the event of war.
Changes were made to existing
staff, and a naval cabinet was
formed in 1889. Proposals were
put forward to build eight
coastal defence battleships over
the next four years (*Siegfried*
class) followed by further
construction if necessary. Two
more vessels were added to the
1890 estimates (*Wörth* class),
but when Rear-Admiral Tirpitz
was appointed Chief of Staff of
the Naval Command in 1892,
and then Secretary of State for
the Navy, he set about the
rebuilding of the German Fleet.
Five ships were laid down to
augment those just completed.
The *Kaiser Friedrich III* class
were perhaps the genesis of
modern German battleships.

GERMAN BATTLESHIPS 1897-1945

R. A. Burt

ARMS AND
ARMOUR

2. *Kaiser Friedrich III* class at sea, *c.* 1900. Their main armament consisted of four 9.4in guns which, although adequate for coastal defence, could not match the more powerful batteries of foreign contemporaries. British Intelligence thought that they were very undergunned for their displacement (10,700 tons), but as the ships had been given a powerful secondary battery of fourteen 5.9in, all mounted in protected positions, considered them adequate for the purpose for which they had been constructed. With their high freeboard forward, they were dry, fair seaboats, but the high and cumbersome superstructure amidships gave them too much topweight and they tended to roll excessively.

3. *Kaiser Barbarossa.* Protection-wise, they were poor even though the main belt was 12 inches thick. The belt was extremely narrow over its entire length and at deep load was completely submerged, leaving the high freeboard hull completely vulnerable to even medium-calibre gunfire from any range. The bottom edge of the belt reduced to 7in and was approximately 3ft 6in below water in the normal load, so that when the ship rolled slightly, or was in a lighter load condition, the edge of the belt was at waterline level. No upper belt was fitted.

INTRODUCTION

First published in Great Britain in
1989 by Arms and Armour Press,
Artillery House, Artillery Row,
London SW1P 1RT.

Distributed in the USA by Sterling
Publishing CP. Inc., 2 Park Avenue,
New York, NY 10016.

Distributed in Australia by
Capricorn Link (Australia) Pty. Ltd.,
P.O. Box 665, Lane Cove, New
South Wales 2066, Australia.

British Library Cataloguing in
Publication Data:
Burt, R. A. (Raymond A.)
German Battleships 1897–1945
1. Germany, Kriegsmarine.
Battleships, 1897–1945
I. Title.   II. Series
623.8'252'0943
ISBN 0-85368-985-7

Line drawings by the author.

Designed and edited by DAG
Publications Ltd. Designed by
David Gibbons; edited by Michael
Boxall; layout by Cilla Eurich;
typeset by Ronset Typesetters Ltd,
Darwen, Lancashire, and by
Typesetters (Birmingham) Limited,
Warley, West Midlands;
camerawork by M&E
Reproductions, North Fambridge,
Essex; printed and bound in Great
Britain by The Alden Press Limited,
Oxford.

As early as 1880 Germany had realized that without a great fleet to control the seas, her powers were limited to the confines of her own boundaries within Europe.

The concept of the modern German Navy dates only from the time of Kaiser Wilhelm II and so it can be classed as a relatively new maritime power. Until about 1880, the only function of the German fleet had been to deter enemy raids on the German coastline, consequently only small coastal defence vessels were built. A newly formed German Naval Command (1889) was well aware that if expansion of territory were required, a large fleet would have to be created to match that of Great Britain and perhaps gain control of the Atlantic and North Sea.

The outbreak of the Boer War and other political incidents at that time prompted the Commander of the German Navy, Admiral Tirpitz, to introduce a Naval Bill doubling the number of battleships in his fleet; then, using the Royal Navy as a model, he started to build a fleet of capital ships which were intended to intimidate Great Britain. This, and the construction of HMS *Dreadnought* in 1906, started one of the most controversial and costly arms races of the century.

During the years leading up to the 1914 war there was intense rivalry – both nations building ship for ship, each larger and more powerful than the last. By August 1914, Germany had the second largest battle fleet in the world, but whether or not it could contain the Royal Navy's mighty squadrons remained to be seen.

The war was a testing ground for designs and gave a chance for all types to justify their existence. The Royal Navy was still numerically superior in capital ships, but, at the beginning of the war, the Germans were not seeking a main battle fleet confrontation. The battles that did take place, however, showed that German ships were second to none, and more than capable of facing any contemporary warship. They were well designed, well armed, well armoured and had speeds to equal most foreign contemporaries. Nevertheless, like Great Britain, Germany learned with dismay that the main lesson of such a war was the enormous cost of sustaining such constant action (average cost for Great Britain was £1,000,000 per day). The resources of both countries were seriously drained. With the end of hostilities in November 1918, the German fleet was interned in Scapa Flow and was scuttled a year later on the orders of the German Commanding Officer, Rear-Admiral Reuter.

For some years after 1919 the Reichsmarine was in turmoil. Morale was low and the ill-disciplined service had only a handful of old pre-dreadnoughts and numerous small craft. Re-organization did not come until the mid-1920s when it was planned to rebuild the fleet, starting with the launching of a cruiser (*Emden*) in 1925. Big ships did not re-appear until 1931, when the innovatory *Deutschland* was launched, because Germany, like the other naval powers, was severely restricted by international naval treaties limiting tonnage to certain displacements for all types of vessels. During the years 1920 to 1930, Great Britain had scrapped many of her own old and newer battleships, but by 1935 wished that they had heeded Admiral David Beatty in 1918 when he said: 'The surrender of the German Fleet has secured the freedom of the seas for such as pass thereon upon their lawful occasions, and is a testimony to the value of seapower which the people of the British Empire will forget at their peril.'

In the late 1930s Germany was in the process of constructing a massive battle fleet, but war broke out before the ships could be completed and she entered the conflict with just seven heavy units. German naval tactics were very different this time; the sinking of merchant shipping being the object rather than confrontation with ships of their own calibre, although when faced with major warships they proved extremely tough antagonists as they had during the first war. Commerce raiding proved most successful and the activities of a few ships kept the Royal Navy extremely busy for almost six years.

It is of interest to note that the major units of the German Fleet never operated as a single fleet or squadron. They were deployed singly or in twos or threes, and there were no fleet actions, as in the war of 1914-18. All the German heavy units were either destroyed at sea or while lying anchored at the end of the war.

▲4

4, 5. *Kaiser Karl der Grosse.* About five years after completion, they were all relegated to subsidiary service ▼5 even though they had undergone some modification to reduce topweight by removing some of the deck levels and 5.9in guns. They were later re-boilered and re-engined and, during the First World War, performed useful service as HQ, Accommodation and POW ships. **4.** shows the ship in Devonport in about 1908. **5.** shows her leaving Kiel.

6. *Mecklenburg.* By increasing displacement another 1,000 tons over KF 111, a more satisfactory design was accomplished in the *Wittelsbach* class of the 1898–1900 estimates. Slight modifications were made and generally they were roomier ships than the preceding classes. As completed, however, they proved to be little more than coastal defence ships, for the simple reason that Germany, at that time, was not interested in increasing displacement and dimensions of her battleships.

7. *Wittelsbach, c.* 1909. They were exceptionally fast ships for their day: *Mecklenburg* made 18 knots with 14,355shp during her preliminary trials. *Wittelsbach* is seen here in Devonport during a German Fleet visit. They were typical German pre-dreadnoughts in appearance, with their tall round funnels, goose-neck cranes, high bridgework, and circular lower masts. Note there are no anti-torpedo nets, unlike other navies' capital ships at this date.

8. *Wettin, c.* 1904-5. By the time the first war had started, all were quite obsolete, but they were retained in service and used as drill and depot ships. (At one time *Mecklenburg* was a prison ship before becoming an accommodation vessel).

6▲   7▼

8▼

▲9 ▼10

▼11

9. *Zähringen*, 1909. Used as a drill ship during the war, *Zähringen* was laid up with the rest of the class to await her fate. She did not follow her sister ships to the scrapyard, however, because in 1926 she was taken off the sale list and converted for use as a radio-controlled target ship. She continued to give good service in this role and survived as late as 1944 – certainly one of the longest life spans of a pre-dreadnought.

10. *Braunschweig*, c. 1910. On an increase of 1,400 tons (over *Wittelsbach* class), German designers were at last able to produce an adequate battleship which compared favourably with some foreign opposition. A slightly shorter and beamier version of *Wittelsbach*, the five *Braunschweig*s were given 11in guns (their first appearance and a marked improvement over the 9.4in of previous classes). Their displacement of 13,200 tons was approaching the maximum (15,000 tons) that German shipyards and docks could handle. The Kiel Canal would need to be dredged if ships became heavier – the main reason why Germany had procrastinated in the matter of increasing displacements.

11. *Hessen*, 1910. The first three-funnelled German pre-dreadnoughts. All served with the High Seas Fleet during the war; *Hessen* was at Jutland in 1916. Note the tall topmasts and aerial spreaders. During their early years they were so alike as to be difficult to distinguish from one another except for the funnel bands.

12. *Elsass, c.* 1910–11. A pre-war view showing her ice-bound during a particularly cold winter. Note the SL positions on tops of main lower top, upper forward platform, upper fore top and small platforms on foremast.

12▲

13. *Hessen,* completely refitted for use as a radio-controlled target ship like the British battleships *Agamemnon* and *Centurion, Hessen* is shown here in that guise. A complete metamorphosis: gone are the three funnels, weather decks, armament and masts. In fact, nothing of her former self remains. Note the large single uptake, tubular foremast, and that all openings such as scuttles, doors, etc., have been filled in.

13▼

▲14

14. *Pommern, c.* 1910. Natural follow-ups to the *Braunschweig* class, and retaining many of their features except that the *Deutschland* class had their upper deck 6.7in guns fitted in casemates rather than turrets. Although British constructors had a healthy respect for this class (all completed from 1906 to 1908) they never saw them as ▼15

true comparisons to the ships that were entering the Royal Navy at that time (*Lord Nelson* and *Dreadnought*, etc.). Germany seems to have ignored the mixed calibre ships which other navies were then building, probably because of the greatly increased displacement involved.

15. *Hannover, c.* 1909. These were the best of the German pre-dreadnoughts and all served in the Great War. Armed with only four 11in guns, however, they were outclassed by practically all other capital ships with the exception of British pre-dreadnoughts which did not usually serve with the Grand Fleet as this class served with

the High Sea Fleet. In most respects, the *Deutschland*s were successful ships and proved to be good gun platforms. Comparable so far as armour was concerned though certainly not armament, were the British *Bulwark* group and perhaps *King Edward VII*.

16. *Schleswig-Holstein*, *c.* 1930. The last German battleships to be completed with large tubular bases around the masts, which always caused unneccessary topweight. They also introduced the half-cased funnel which was to become a familiar German fitting over the next ten years.

All five *Deutschland*s were at Jutland; *Pommern* blew up from a torpedo hit which sparked off the magazines.

17. *Schlesien*, May 1937, port quarter view. After the war *Hannover*, *Schleswig-Holstein* and *Schlesien* were reconstructed, the latter two receiving considerable improvements. Their funnels were trunked together, altering their appearance drastically. *Hannover* ceased to be an active unit in 1935, but the other two entered the Second World War as fighting units – *Schleswig-* *Holstein* firing the first shots of the war on 1 September 1939. Although not considered suitable for general sea-going tasks, they were of excellent value as coastal defence ships and for shore bombardment.

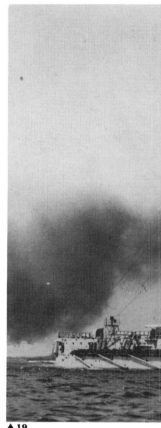

19. *Nassau*, 1912. The Germans took their time when designing their first all big-gunned battleship; the final layout was chosen from at least a dozen sketches. The decision to go over to the type, incidentally, was a contributory cause in the enlarging of the Kaiser Wilhelm Canal, Wilhelmshaven dockyard and docking accommodation. A great advance in displacement over preceding classes, the *Nassau* class were severely criticized for the siting of their big guns. Although having two more guns than the British *Dreadnought*, they could still only bring the same number to bear on any broadside. Internally, because of the large number of turrets, they were terribly cramped and the weight of the midship turrets made them roll considerably; it was reported that while on trials *Nassau* rolled to an extremely dangerous degree.

20. *Rheinland* as completed, 1910. Apart from their poor sea-keeping qualities, they were generally fair ships for a first attempt and were well armed and armoured. Unlike the British *Dreadnought*, they were fitted with reciprocating engines and proved to be somewhat slower and less reliable than the British ships. In displacement, however, they were on a par with the *Bellerophon* class with

▲19
a 6in wider beam and one foot less draught. Accommodation was extremely poor in the German ships.

21. *Westfalen*, 1909–10. Note W/T gaffs and no anti-torpedo

▲18
18. *Schlesien*, winter 1942. Seen here when she was being used as an ice-breaker in the
▼20

Baltic during 1942. Note that she is camouflaged in a bizarre scheme of at least four colours.

nets. Early sketch designs show one particular layout with twin lattice or lattice-type masts, which suggests that an eye was being kept on the American Navy at that time. As completed, however, they were fitted with single poles forward and aft, and goose-necked cranes amidships to handle the boats. The ships were not easy to distinguish one from another, but there were small differences such as *Nassau* and *Westfalen* having tall, angled W/T masts whereas the other two had none. Also, *Nassau*'s cranes had small fittings on the elbow. Funnel bands were painted up, but were liable to frequent change – as was the case with early British Fleet markings.

▲ 22   ▼ 23

▼ 24

22. *Rheinland*, 1912. All the ships of the class were present at Jutland, some of them being hit by shells and sustaining superficial damage. One of their early tasks had been to support the battlecruisers when they bombarded Lowestoft and Yarmouth on 24 April 1916, and cover their exit routes when they withdrew. *Nassau*'s secondary armament was considerably superior to that of the early British *Dreadnought*s (twelve 5.9in against 12pdrs or 4in guns).

23. *Westfalen* in 1921 at Birkenhead, Merseyside, awaiting the scrapper's torch. At the end of the war they were not part of the great German fleet that sailed into Scapa Flow in 1918, but were treated individually and stayed in Germany until allocated as 'war prizes', *Nassau* to Japan, *Posen* and *Westfalen* to Great Britain. *Rheinland*, however, had run aground on 9 July 1918 and was later scrapped in Dordrecht.

24. *Von der Tann*, amidships, 1911. She introduced large turbines into the German Navy and proved an exceptionally fast ship on her preliminary trials. In construction, there was a general striving to save weight which resulted in lighter framing than the usual British practice for such warships. On her early gunnery trials the blast from the 11in guns shook her hull badly. Designed by constructor, K. Konow, she was, nevertheless, a match for any of the 12in-gunned British battlecruisers. Note large ventilation grids, boat-handling derricks and 5.9in guns are all amidships.

25. *Von der Tann* at the Coronation Fleet Review in 1911. Germany's answer to the battlecruiser *Invincible* was viewed with much interest by British naval constructors, and made a big impact at the Fleet Review at Spithead. She completely outclassed *Invincible* following *Indefatigable* regarding armour protection in all areas. *Von der Tann* was fitted with Frahm's anti-rolling tanks after construction was well advanced, mainly because of the poor performance of the *Nassau* group when caught in a swell in the North Sea.

26. *Von der Tann*, 1911. A strange juxtaposition when she was representing the German Navy at the Coronation Review in Britain and sat alongside the battleships *St Vincent*, *Vanguard* and the battlecruiser *Indefatigable*.

▲27

27. *Von der Tann*, 21 November 1918. Seen here shortly after arriving in Scapa Flow to be interned. Note how little she has changed since the 1911 photographs. Although the oldest of the German battlecruisers, she still saw much action during the war and ▼28 battle time at Lowestoft Scarborough, Whitby, Yarmouth and Jutland were all recorded. At Jutland she hit and sank *Indefatigable* in about twelve minutes.

28. *Ostfriesland*. Basically an improved *Nassau*, by increasing dimensions, machinery installation and gun size up to 12in. On an increase of 3,500 tons it became possible to improve armour thickness and distribution, but the gun positions of the *Nassau* group were repeated, and they suffered in the same way by not being able to bring more than eight guns to bear on any broadside. In comparison with *Nassau*, they were good gun platforms and very steady ships; accommodation-wise, however, they were terribly cramped owing to the numerous turrets.

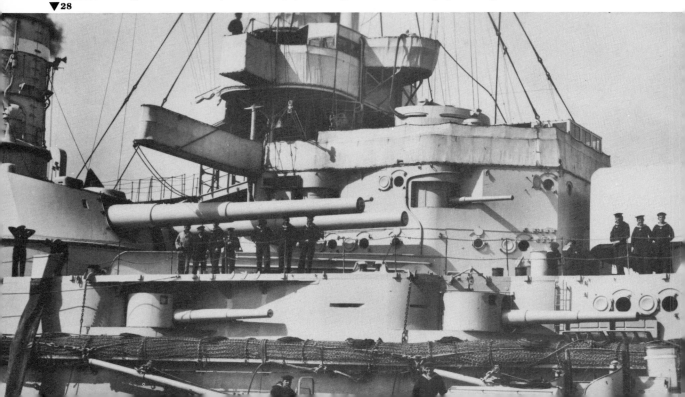

29▲

29. *Helgoland*. Like *Von der Tann*, the *Helgoland* class had Frahm's anti-rolling tanks built into them and these coupled with the longer, beamier hull made them more suitable for heavy seas. They were the only German dreadnoughts with three funnels.

30. *Thüringen*. All ships of the class were at Jutland in 1916, but none was badly damaged. Throughout the war they played their part in support of the battlecruisers and often showed their worth. At the end of the war they were not sent for internment in Scapa Flow, but were allocated as war prizes. *Ostfriesland* made headlines when, after being sent to the USA, she was subject to aerial attacks from Billy Mitchell in an effort to prove that the day of the battleship was over. The tests, however, did not prove this, but rather that the day of the attack aircraft had not arrived.

31. *Moltke* on trials making 28 knots with 85,780shp. Although very like *Von der Tann*, the length was increased which made it possible to add another turret at the after end of the ship. This extra turret was the

30▲

first superimposed fitting in the German Navy. As completed, they represented the best of their type to date. They were splendid-looking ships with their high freeboard forward, limited bridgework, large rounded funnels and twin pole masts.

31▼

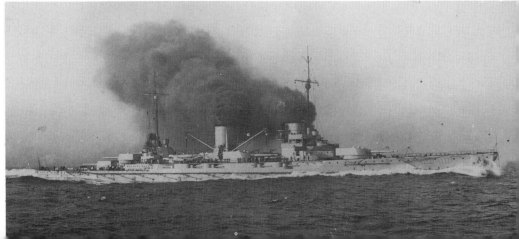

▲32

32. *Goeben*. She saw plenty of
action, having been fired on by
the cruiser *Gloucester* in August
1914 for a start. In October of
the same year she sank the
Russian minelayer *Prut*; carried
out numerous bombardment
duties; saw action against the
Russian battleship *Svjatoj-
Evstafij* and was hit by two
mines in December 1914. She
was not present at Jutland in
1916. She saw out the war in
the Turkish Navy, having been
sent to encourage that country
to fight against Britain.

33. *Moltke*. During operations
in the Gulf of Riga on 19 August
1915 *Moltke* was torpedoed in
the starboard bow by the British
submarine *E1*. Although
seriously damaged, her internal
bulkheads held up and she was
able to dock with 450 tons of
water inside her. The
photograph shows her in dry
dock for repairs.

34. *Yavuz*, 1936. Officially
handed over to Turkey in 1918
and renamed *Jawas Selim*, she
lay idle for many years after
undergoing a refit, and did not
become active again until 1930.
Renamed *Yavuz* in 1936 she saw
no action during the Second

World War and was laid up in
1948. During this period there
were virtually no appearance
changes except for the
mainmast being removed in
1941/2 to give the small guns a
better arc of fire.

35. *Yavuz*, 1970. On the sale list
from 1963, she holds the record
as the longest surviving
dreadnought. She lay as a
museum ship for years, being
looked after by a single
watchman and his cat. West
Germany did try to purchase

her as a Museum Ship and as
the last surviving German
dreadnought, but for some
strange reason the offer was
refused and, sadly, she was
scrapped in 1971–4.

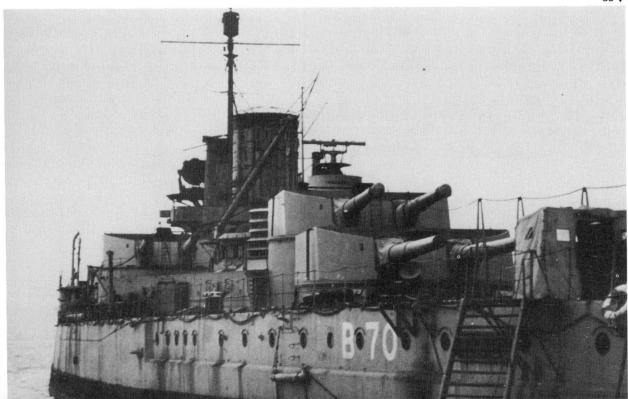

▲36 ▼37

36. *Kaiser*. A very marked improvement over the preceding classes, the *Kaiser*s represented the foundation on which future German battleships would be built. In most respects, they were a battleship version of *Moltke*

with a similar gun layout, less SHP and considerably more protection. The chief innovation of the class was that they were fitted with turbines for the first time in a German battleship. They also sported supplementary oil sprayers on the boilers so that the achieving of their designed speed (21 knots) was much easier than in preceding classes.

37. *Prinzregent Luitpold*. During the preliminary layout stage, it was thought possible that she might be fitted with diesel propulsion, but this never came about and she received only two normal turbines instead of three like her sisters. As a result she remained the slowest of the class.

38. *Friedrich der Grosse*. In appearance, they were very different from other German battleships, but as a class were very difficult to distinguish one from another. Small differences were apparent in the steam pipes on funnels, bridgework, masts and SL arrangements. Rather stark-looking vessels, they were the last German battleships to have the midships guns *en echelon* which were always hampered with regard to arcs of fire.

39. *König*. Developed from the *Kaiser* group, the four *König*s reflected many improvements and, other than the following *Baden* and *Bayern*, were the best German battleships of the Second World War. They were

often criticized for retaining a 12in calibre gun; it was felt that an increase could have been made before the *Bayern* class was completed, which would have equipped the German Navy with four 15in-gunned ships at Jutland. The principal feature of the design, however, was the twin superimposed turrets forward and aft, as in British practice. This did away with the need for central location, and the hull compartmentation was made more secure. The protection was more than adequate for a World War One design, and their speed was approximately equal to most rivals.

KAISER FRIEDRICH III CLASS

Displacement
10,790 tons normal load

Dimensions
Length: 384ft (wl)
Beam: 65ft 6in
Draught: 27ft.

Builders
Kaiser Friedrich III Wilhelmshaven DVOCKYARD, LAID DOWN +—&:
LAUNCHED +
July 1896; completed 1898.
Kaiser Wilhelm der Grosse Germania Shipyard, laid down 1896; launched 1 June 1899; completed 1900.
Kaiser Wilhelm II Wilhelmshaven Dockyard, laid down 1898; launched 14 September 1897; completed 1899.
Kaiser Karl der Grosse Blohm & Voss Shipyard, laid down 1898; launched 18 October 1899; completed 1900.
Kaiser Barbarossa Schichau Werke, laid down 1898; launched 21 April 1900; completed 1901.

Armament
4×9.4in 40cal
14×5.9in 40cal (*Kaiser Barbarossa* 18×5.9in)
12×3.4in
12×1pdr
8 MG
TT: 6×17.7in (submerged).

Armour
main belt: 12in—4in
Bulkheads: 8in
Barbettes: 10in
Turrets: 10in faces
Conning tower: 10in
Decks: 3in main
Casemates: 6in.

Machinery
Three sets 3-cylinder triple-expansion engines driving three screws, eight cylindrical and four Schulz boilers in first three, six cylindrical in others.

Designed SHP
14,000 for 18 knots.

Fuel
650—1,050 tons coal plus 100 tons oil.

Complement
658—687.

Fates
Kaiser Friedrich III scrapped from 1920.
Kaiser Wilhelm II scrapped from 1921.
Kaiser Barbarossa scrapped from 1920.
Kaiser Wilhelm der Grosse scrapped from 1920.
Kaiser Karl der Grosse scrapped from 1920.

WITTELSBACH CLASS

Displacement
11,830 tons normal load; 12,553 tons full load.

Dimensions
Length: 400ft (wl)
Beam: 67ft
Draught: 27/28ft.

Builders
Wittelsbach Wilhelmshaven Shipyard, laid down September 1898; launched 7 October 1900; completed 1902.
Mecklenburg Vulkan, laid down May 1900; launched 9 November 1901; completed 1903.
Wettin Schichau, laid down October 1899; launched 6 June 1901; completed 1902.
Zähringen Germania Shipyard, laid down November 1899; launched 12 June 1901; completed 1902.
Schwaben Wilhelmshaven Shipyard, laid down November 1900; launched 19 August 1901; completed 1903.

Armament
4×9.4in 40cal
18×5.9in
12×3in
8 MG
TT: 5×17.7in.

Armour (Krupp)
Main belt: 9in amidships, 4in ends
Barbettes: 10in
Turrets: 10in faces
Battery: 5in
Conning tower: 10in face
Decks: 3in on slopes.

Machinery
Three sets vertical triple-expansion engines driving three screws, six cylindrical and six Schulz-Thornycroft boilers.

Designed SHP
15,000 for 18 knots.

Fuel
653/1,400 tons coal plus 200 tons oil.

Complement
650.

Fates
Wittelsbach broken up 1921.
Mecklenburg scrapped 1921.
Wettin scrapped 1922
Zähringen bombed and sunk by aircraft 18 December 1944.
Schwaben scrapped 1921.

BRAUNSCHWEIG CLASS

Displacement
13,200 tons normal load; 14,600 tons full load.

Dimensions
Length: 398ft 6in pp; 410ft wl; 430ft oa
Beam: 72ft
Draught: 25ft 9in—28ft.

Builders
Braunschweig Krupp Shipyard, laid down 1901; launched 20 December 1902; completed 1904.
Hessen Krupp Shipyard, laid down 1902; launched 18 September 1903; completed 1905.
Preussen Vulkan Werke, laid down 1902; launched 30 October 1903; completed 1905.
Elsass Schichau Werke, laid down 1901; launched 26 March 1903; completed 1904.
Lothringen Schichau Werke, laid down 1902; launched 27 March 1904; completed 1906.

Armament
4×11in 40cal
14×6.7in 40cal
14×3.4in
12×1pdr
8 MG
TT: 6×17.7in (5 submerged, 1 above water).

Armour (Krupp)
Main belt: 9in, 4in ends
Bulkheads: 8in
Barbettes: 11in sides
Turrets: ·11in faces
Secondary battery: 6in
Conning tower: 12in
Decks: 3in main.

Machinery
Three sets 3-cylinder vertical inverted triple-expansion engines driving three screws, eight Schulz and six cylindrical boilers.

Designed SHP
16,000 for 18 knots.

Fuel
700 tons coal normal, 1,600 tons max. plus 200 tons oil.

Complement
691—732.

Fates

Braunschweig scrapped from 1932.
Elsass scrapped from 1932.
Lothringen scrapped from 1931
Preussen scrapped from 1931 except midships section.
Hessen handed over to Russian Navy in 1945. Fate unknown but probably scrapped.

DEUTSCHLAND CLASS

Displacement
13,200 tons normal load; 14,300 tons deep load.

Dimensions
Length: 410ft wl; 419ft 6in oa
Beam: 72ft
Draught: 25ft 5in mean.

Builders
Deutschland Krupp Shipyard, laid down June 1903; launched 19 November 1904; completed 1906.
Hannover Wilhelmshaven Shipyard, laid down November 1904; launched 29 September 1905; completed 1907.
Pommern Vulkan, laid down April 1904; launched 2 December 1905; completed 1907.
Schleswig-Holstein Schichau, laid down August 1905; launched 7 December 1906; completed 1908.
Schlesien Krupp Shipyard, laid down 1905; launched 28 May 1906; completed 1908.

Armament
4 × 11in 40cal
14 × 6.7in
20 × 24pdr
4 MG
TT: 6 × 17.7in submerged.

Armour (Krupp)
Main belt: 9½in—8in, ends 4in
Barbettes: 11in
Turrets: 10in faces
Battery: 6½in
Casemates: 6½in
Conning tower: 2in
Decks: 3in on slopes.

Machinery
Three sets 3-cylinder vertical triple-expansion engines driving three screws, twelve Schulz-Thornycroft boilers.

Designed SHP
16,000 for 18 knots.

Fuel
800 tons coal normal; 1,800 tons max. plus 200 tons oil.

Complement
730.

Fates
Deutschland scrapped 1920.
Hannover scrapped 1920.
Pommern sunk by torpedoes at Jutland June 1916.
Schleswig-Holstein bombed and badly damaged 18 December 1944 and scuttled 21 March 1945.
Schlesien mined 3 May 1945 and scuttled next day.

NASSAU CLASS

Displacement
18,600 tons as designed; 18,569 tons load condition; 20,210 tons deep load.

Dimensions
Length: 451ft 9in pp; 478ft wl
Beam: 88ft 4in
Draught: 26ft 7in mean as designed.

Builders
Nassau Wilhelmshaven Shipyard, laid down 22 July 1907; launched 7 March 1908; completed 1 October 1909.
Westfalen A. G. Weser Shipyard, laid down December 1908; launched 1 July 1909; completed 16 November 1909.
Posen Germania Shipyard, Kiel, laid down 11 June 1907; launched 12 December 1908; completed 31 May 1910.
Rheinland Vulkan Werke, Stettin, laid down 1 June 1907; launched 26 September 1908; completed 30 April 1910.

Armament
12 × 11in 45cal (in electrically controlled turrets)
12 × 5.9in 45cal
16 × 3.4in 45cal
2 × 7pdr
2 MG
TT: 6 × 17.7in (submerged).

Armour (Krupp)
Main belt: 11.42in tapering to 4¾in at lower edge; 6in forward, 4in aft
Bulkheads: 7¾in
Barbettes: 11in—8in
Turrets: 11in faces
Battery: 6½in closed by 6½in bulkheads
Conning tower: 12in sides with 16in strake at fore
Aft conning tower: 8in—12in
Torpedo builkheads: 1⅛in—1in
Decks: extended the whole length of vessel with 2in on flat, and 3in on slopes.

Machinery
Three vertical triple-expansion engines driving three screws, all in separate watertight compartments and all situated under the mainmast, twelve Schulz naval boilers in three separate transverse rooms.

Designed SHP
20,000 for 19 to 20 knots.

Fuel
935 tons coal normal; 2,658 tons coal max. plus 197 tons oil.

Radius
3,540 nm at 18 knots; 8,000 nm at 10 knots.

Complement
966 as private ship; 1,008 in wartime.

Fates
Nassau scrapped in Holland 1920.
Westfalen scrapped at Birkenhead 1924.
Posen scrapped at Dordrecht 1921.
Rheinland scrapped at Dordrecht 1921.

HELGOLAND CLASS

Displacement
22,440 tons as designed; 25,000 tons deep load.

Dimensions
Length: 546ft 3in wl
Beam: 93ft 6in
Draught: 26ft 11in mean.

Builders
Helgoland Howalds Werke, Kiel, laid down 24 December 1908; launched 25 September 1909; completed 19 December 1911.
Ostfriesland Wilhelmshaven Shipyard, laid down 19 October 1908; launched 30 September 1909; completed 1 August 1911.
Thuringen Weser Shipyard, Bremen, laid down 7 November 1908; launched 27 November 1909; completed 1 July 1911.
Oldenburg Schichau Werke, laid down 1 March 1909; launched 30 June 1910; completed 1 May 1912.

Armament
12 × 12in 45cal in six twin turrets
14 × 5.9in 45cal
14 × 22pdr 45cal
2 × 7pdr
2 MG
TT: 6 × 19.7in (submerged).

Armour (Krupp)
Main belt: 8in tapering to 7¾in at lower deck level

Total height of protective belt: 16ft; ends 7¾in (forward and aft)
Bulkheads: 7¾in
Barbettes: 11¾in
Turrets: 11¾in faces
Battery: 7¾in
Conning tower: 12in with 16in portion at face
Aft conning tower: 7¾in
Anti-torpedo bulkheads: 1½in
Decks: Principal armoured deck 1½in with 2¾in on slopes.

Machinery
Three vertical 4-cylinder triple expansion engines driving three screws, fifteen Schulz boilers (210psi) in three separate compartments.

Designed SHP
25,000 for 21 knots.

Fuel
886 tons coal normal, 2,950 tons max.

Radius
2,950 nm at 18 knots; 7,200 nm at 10 knots.

Complement
1,106 as private ship; 1,097 normal.

Fates
Helgoland scrapped at Morecambe 1924.
Ostfriesland sunk as target in USA 21 July 1921.
Thuringen scrapped at Lorient 1923.
Oldenburg scrapped at Dordrecht 1920/21.

VON DER TANN

Displacement
19,100 tons load; 21,082 tons full load.

Dimensions
Length: 562ft 8in wl; 563ft oa
Beam: 87ft 3in
Draught: 26ft 7in mean.

Builder
Blohm & Voss Shipyard, laid down 25 March 1908; launched 20 March 1909; completed 1 September 1910.

Armament
8×11in 45cal mounted on Drehscheiben-Lafette C/06 type, in pairs
10×5.9in 45cal on CP mountings C/02/06 in central battery
16×22pdr 45cal semi-automatic
2×7pdr
2 MG
TT: 4×17.7in (submerged).

Armour (Krupp)
Main belt: 9.84in; ends 6in and 4in

Bulkheads: 7in—4in
Barbettes: 9in
Turrets: 9in faces, 3in roofs
Battery: 6in
Casemates: 1in
Anti-torpedo bulkheads: 1in
Decks: 3in—2in—1in.

Machinery
Two sets Parsons turbines driving four screws, eighteen Schulz-Thornycroft boilers in three sets (6 in each).

Designed SHP
41,000 for 24/25 knots.

Fuel
984 tons coal normal; 2,760 tons max. plus 200 tons oil.

Radius
2,500 nm at 22 knots.

Complement
911 as private ship; 1,000 during wartime.

Fate
Scuttled at Scapa Flow June 1919; raised and scrapped during the early 1930s.

MOLTKE CLASS

Displacement
22,616 tons normal; 25,200 tons deep load.

Dimensions
Length: 610ft 3in wl; 612ft oa
Beam: 96ft 9in
Draught: 27ft mean.

Builders
Moltke Blohm & Voss Shipyard, laid down 7 December 1908; launched 7 April 1910; completed 30 September 1911.
Goeben Blohm & Voss Shipyard, laid down 28 August 1909; launched 28 February 1911; completed 2 July 1912.

Armament
10×11in 45cal in twin Drehscheiben-Lafette C/08 mountings
12×5.9in 45cal
12×3.4in
2 MG
TT: 4×19.7in (submerged).

Armour
Main belt: 10¾in tapering to 5in at lower edge
Upper belt: 8in
Ends: 4¾in
Bulkheads: 8in
Barbettes: 9in—8in
Turrets: 9in faces, 3½in—2in roofs

Anti-torpedo bulkheads: 2in—1⅛in
Decks: 3in—2in—1in.

Machinery
Two sets Parsons turbines driving four screws, twenty-four Schulz-Thornycroft boilers (235psi).

Designed SHP
52,000 for 25½ knots.

Fuel
984 tons coal normal; 2,952 tons max. plus 200 tons oil.

Radius
2,350 nm at 22/23 knots.

Fates
Moltke scuttled at Scapa Flow June 1919; raised and scrapped during late 1920s.
Goeben Taken over by Turkish Navy and not scrapped until 1971.

KAISER CLASS

Displacement
24,310—24,410 tons normal; 26,580 tons full load.

Dimensions
Length: 546ft 4in wl
Beam: 95ft 3in
Draught: 27ft 3in normal, 28ft 9in full load (mean).

Builders
Kaiser Imperial Dockyard, Kiel, laid down October 1909; launched 22 March 1911; completed 1 August 1912.
Friedrich der Grosse Vulkan Werke, laid down 26 January 1910; launched June 1911; completed 15 October 1912.
Kaiserin Howalds Werke, laid down November 1910; launched 11 November 1911; completed 14 May 1913.
König Albert Schichau Werke, laid down 17 July 1910; launched 27 April 1912; completed 31 July 1913.
Prinzregent Luitpold Germania Shipyard, laid down 1911; launched 17 December 1912; completed 19 August 1913.

Armament
10×12in 50cal in five twin turrets with some electric machinery
14×5.9in 45cal
12×22pdr
4×12pdr
2 MG
TT: 5×19.7in (submerged).

Armour (Krupp)
Main belt: 13.78in
Bulkheads: 7¾in

Barbettes: 11¾in
Turrets: 11¾in–11in
Conning tower: 13½in
Aft conning tower: 7¾in
Anti-torpedo bulkheads: 1¾in–1¼in
Main armoured deck: 1¼in on flat, 4in on slopes.

Machinery
Three sets of turbines (two in *Prinzregent Luitpold*) driving three screws, sixteen Schulz-Thornycroft boilers (14 in PL).

Designed SHP
28,000 for 21/22 knots.

Fuel
984 tons coal normal, 3,543 tons max. plus 197 tons oil.

Radius
3,920 nm at 19 knots; 6,450 nm at 10 knots.

Complement
1,125 as private ship.

Fates
Kaiser scuttled in Scapa Flow 21 June 1919.
Prinzregent Luitpold scuttled in Scapa Flow 21 June 1919.
Kaiserin scuttled in Scapa Flow 21 June 1919.
König Albert scuttled in Scapa Flow 21 June 1919.
Friedrich der Grosse scuttled in Scapa Flow 21 June 1919.
All raised and scrapped during the 1930s.

SEYDLITZ

Displacement
24,610 tons normal; 28,500 tons full load.

Dimensions
Length: 656ft 2in wl; 658ft oa
Beam: 93ft 6in
Draught: 27ft normal; 30ft full load.

Builder
Blohm & Voss, laid down 4 December 1911; launched 30 March 1912; completed 22 May 1913.

Armament
10×11in 50cal in twin mountings
12×5.9in 45cal
12×3.45in
TT: 4×19.7in (submerged).

Armour (Krupp)
Main belt: 12in
Ends: 4in
Upper belt: 4in

Citadel armour: 10½in
Armoured bulkheads: 8in–6in–4in
Barbettes: 10in–9in–1½in
Turrets: 10in faces, 8in sides, 4in–2¼in roofs
Conning tower: 14in–10in
Aft conning tower: 8in–2in
Anti-torpedo bulkheads: 2in–1½in
5.9in casemates: 6in
Upper deck: 1in
Armoured deck: 3in–1¼in on flat; 2in on slopes.

Machinery
Two sets Parsons-type turbines driving four screws, twenty-seven Schulz naval boilers in five compartments.

Designed SHP
67,000 for 26.5 knots.

Fuel
984 tons coal min.; 3,543 tons max. plus 200 tons oil.

Radius
4,020 nm at 15/16 knots.

Complement
1,068.

Fate
Scuttled in Scapa Flow 21 June 1919; raised 1928 and scrapped.

KÖNIG CLASS

Displacement
25,390 tons normal; 27,500 tons deep load.

Dimensions
Length: 573ft 2in wl
Beam: 96ft 9in
Draught: 27ft 3in normal (mean).

Builders
König Wilhelmshaven Shipyard, laid down October 1911; launched 1 March 1913; completed 26 August 1914.
Grosser Kurfürst Vulkan Werke, laid down October 1911; launched 5 May 1913; completed 19 August 1914.
Markgraf Weser Shipyard, laid down November 1911; launched 4 June 1913; completed 1 October 1914.
Kronprinz Germania Shipyard, laid down 8 May 1912; launched 21 February 1914; completed 8 November 1914.

Armament
10×12in 50cal
14×5.9in 45cal
6×22pdr
TT: 5×19.7in (submerged).

Armour (Krupp)
Main belt: 14in extending from 'A' to 'Y'

barbettes
Ends: 6in
Bulkheads: 10in
Barbettes: 10in
Turrets: 14in faces
Conning tower: 14in face and sides
Aft conning tower: 10in
Decks: 2½in on flat, 3in on slopes.

Machinery
Three triple acting Parsons-type turbines driving three screws, twelve Schulz naval-type boilers (coal) and three oil-fired boilers.

Designed SHP
31,000 for 21 knots.

Fuel
984 tons coal; 689 tons oil.

Radius
8,000 nm at 12 knots.

Complement
1,130.

Fates
König scuttled in Scapa Flow 21 June 1919.
Grosser Kurfürst scuttled in Scapa Flow 21 June 1919.
Markgraf scuttled in Scapa Flow 21 June 1919.
Kronprinz scuttled in Scapa Flow 21 June 1919.

Kronprinz was raised and scrapped in 1936, but the others were not touched until 1962.

DERFFLINGER CLASS

Displacement
26,180 tons normal (*Derfflinger*); 26,318 tons normal (*Lützow*); 30,707 tons full load.

Dimensions
Length: 686ft wl; 690ft 3in oa
Beam: 95ft 1½in oa
Draught: 27ft 6in normal; 30ft full load.

Builders
Derfflinger Blohm & Voss, laid down January 1912; launched 12 July 1913; completed 1 September 1914.
Lützow Schichau Werke, laid down July 1912; launched 29 November 1913; completed 8 August 1915.

Armament
8×12in 50cal in twin mountings
12×5.9in 45cal
4×3.45in
TT: 4×19.7in.

Armour (Krupp)
Main belt: 12in
Lower belt: 4in
Upper belt: 6in
Bulkheads: 10in–8in
Barbettes: 10¼in–4in
Turrets: 10½in faces, 8¾in sides,
4¼in–3¼in roofs
Anti-torpedo bulkheads: 1½in
Conning tower: 14in–8in
Aft conning tower: 8in–2in
Superstructure deck: 2in–1¼in
Main armoured deck: 3¼in–2in–1¼in.

Machinery
Two Parsons-type turbines driving four
screws, fourteen Schulz naval coal-fired
boilers, plus four oil-fired boilers.

Designed SHP
63,000 for 26.5 knots.

Fuel
738 tons coal normal, 246 tons oil
normal; 3,642 tons coal, 984 tons oil
max.

Radius
5,300 nm at 14/15 knots.

Complement
1,112–1,182.

Fates
Derfflinger scuttled in Scapa Flow 21
June 1919. Raised and scrapped 1934/6.
Lützow sunk in action 31 May 1916
(Jutland).

HINDENBURG

Displacement
26,513 tons normal; 31,000 tons full
load.

Dimensions
Length: 697ft wl; 698ft oa
Beam: 95ft
Draught: 28ft normal; 31ft 6in full load.

Builder
Wilhelmshaven Shipyard, laid down 30
June 1913; launched 1 August 1915;
completed 10 May 1917.

Armament
8×12in 50cal in twin mountings
12×5in 45cal
4×3.4in
TT: 4×23.6in (submerged).

Armour (Krupp)
Main belt: 12in
Upper belt: 8¾in
Otherwise as *Derfflinger*.

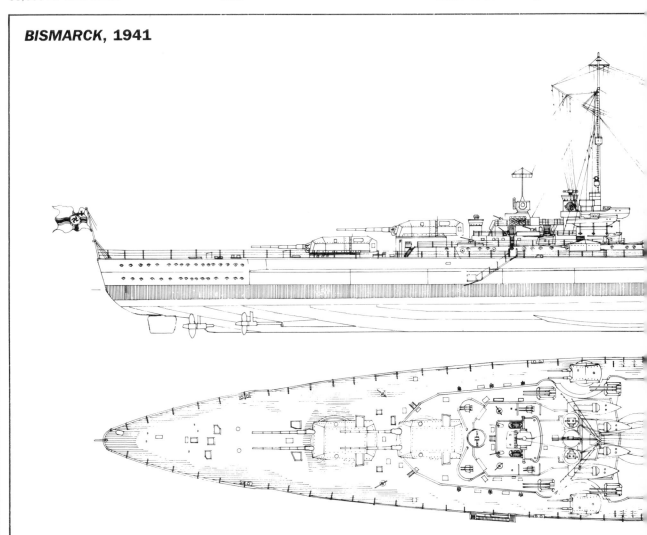

BISMARCK, 1941

Machinery
As *Derfflinger*, but boilers and compartments re-arranged.

Designed SHP
72,000 for 27 knots.

Fuel
As *Derfflinger*.

Radius
As *Derfflinger*.

Complement
1,180.

Fate
Scuttled in Scapa Flow 21 June 1919; raised and scrapped 1930/2.

BAYERN CLASS

Displacement
28,000 tons normal; 31,800 tons full load.

DVIMENSIONS
Length: 560ft 6in wl; 589ft 10in oa
Beam: 99ft
Draught: 27ft 9in normal; 31ft full load.

Builders
Bayern Howalds Werke, laid down 20 September 1913; launched 18 February 1915; completed March 1916.
Baden Schichau Shipyard, laid down 29 March 1913; launched 30 October 1915; completed October 1916.

Armament
8×15in 45cal Mk 1 in twin mountings
16×5.9in 45cal
4×3.45in
TT: 5×23.6in (submerged).

Armour (Krupp)
Main belt: 14in
Ends: 8in–6in
Upper belt: 10in
Lower belt: 6½in
Armoured citadel: 10in
Barbettes: 14in
Turrets: 14in faces, 10in sides, 11½in rears, 8in sloping roofs, 4in roofs on flat
Anti-torpedo bulkheads: 3in–2in
Conning tower: 14in face plates
Aft conning tower: 6½in
Superstructure deck: 1½in
Main deck: 4¾in–1¼in at stern, 1¼in slopes.

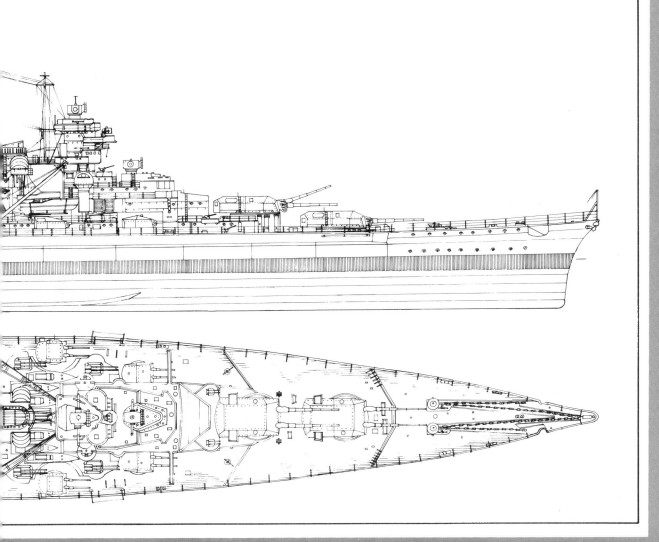

Machinery
Three sets Parsons turbines driving three screws, fourteen Schulz naval boilers in nine compartments (three oil burning).

Designed SHP
34,000 for 21 knots.

Fuel
886 tons coal plus 197 tons oil normal; 3,346 tons coal plus 610 tons oil max.

Radius
5,000 nm at 12 knots.

Fates
Bayern scuttled in Scapa Flow June 21 1919.
Baden attempted scuttle foiled and beached by tugs. Later used for experiments and finally, on 16 August 1921, sunk as target by British battleships (15in guns).

DEUTSCHLAND CLASS

Displacement
11,700 tons normal; 15,900 tons deep load (*Deutschland* and *Scheer*); 12,100 tons normal; 16,200 tons deep load (*Graf Spee*).

Dimensions
Length: 593ft pp; 609ft 4in wl; 616ft 9in oa
Beam: 67ft 6in (*Deutschland*); 69ft 6in (*Scheer*); 71ft 4in (*Graf Spee*).
Draught: 21ft mean normal load; 24ft deep load.

Builders
Deutschland Deutsche Werke, laid down 5 February 1929; launched 19 May 1931; completed 1 April 1933.
Admiral Scheer Wilhelmshaven Shipyard, laid down 1 October 1932; launched 30 June 1934; completed 6 January 1936.
Admiral Graf Spee Wilhelmshaven Shipyard, laid down 25 June 1931; launched 1 April 1933; completed 12 November 1934.

Armament
6×11in 55.4cal in triple mountings
8×5.9in 55cal in single mounts
6×3.45in
TT: 8×21in (above water).

Armour (Krupp)
Main belt: 2⅜in (*Deutschland* and *Scheer*); 3¼in *Graf Spee*
Barbettes: 4in
Turrets: 5½in–3⅜in
Conning tower: 6in
Aft conning tower: 2in
Anti-torpedo bulkheads: 1¾in

(*Deutschland*); 1⅝in (*Scheer* and *Graf Spee*)
Decks: 1¾in–1⅝in

Machinery
Four M.A.N. 9-cylinder double-acting 2-stroke diesel engines driving two screws.

Designed SHP
54,000 for 26 knots.

Fuel
2,854 tons oil.

Radius
19,000–20,000 nm at 10 knots.

Complement
619–1,150.

Fates
Deutschland badly damaged by 5.5-ton bombs 16 April 1945 then scuttled 4 May 1945.
Admiral Scheer sunk by British bombers 9 April 1945.
Admiral Graf Spee scuttled outside Montevideo 17 December 1939.

SCHARNHORST CLASS

Displacement
34,841 tons normal; 38,900 tons deep load.

Dimensions
Length: 741ft 6in wl; 771ft oa
Beam: 100ft
Draught: 27ft normal; 32ft 6in max.

Builders
Scharnhorst Wilhelmshaven Shipyard, laid down 16 May 1935; launched 3 October 1936; completed 7 January 1939.
Gneisenau Deutsche Werke, Kiel, laid down March 1935; launched 8 December 1936; completed 21 May 1938.

Armament
9×11in 55.4cal in triple mountings
12×5.9in 55cal in double mountings
14×3.45in 65cal
16×37mm AA
10×20mm AA
TT: 6×21in above water.

Armour (Krupp)
Main belt: 14in
Forward belt: 5in
Aft belt: 3in
Upper belt: 10in
Lower belt: 6½in
Barbettes: 14in–8in
Turrets: 14in faces, 11in sides, 9¾in rears, 6in crown
Secondary turrets: 6in faces

Secondary barbettes: 6in
Conning tower: 14in
Aft conning tower: 4in
Anti-torpedo bulkhead: 1½in
Armoured deck: 2in–¾in, 4in slopes.

Machinery
Three Brown Boveri (*Gneisenau* Germania) turbines driving three screws, twelve Wagner extra high-pressure boilers in three compartments.

Designed SHP
165,000 for 32 knots.

Fuel
2,756 tons oil min.; 6,200 tons max.

Radius
8,800 nm at 19 knots; 10,000 nm at 16½ knots.

Complement
1,669–1,840.

Fates
Scharnhorst sunk in classic surface action by *Duke of York* (14in shells) and torpedoes from other ships.
Gneisenau constantly damaged by bombs in dock during 1941–2 and never went to sea again. Finally scuttled 27 March 1945.

BISMARCK CLASS

Displacement
41,700 tons light; 45,172 tons normal; 50,995¾ tons extra deep (*Bismarck*). 42,900 tons light; 46,400 tons normal; 52,600 tons deep load (*Tirpitz*).

Dimensions
Length: 794ft wl; 822ft 9in oa (*Bismarck*); 798ft wl; 828ft oa (*Tirpitz*)
Beam: 118ft 4in (*Bismarck*); 119ft (*Tirpitz*)
Draught: 28ft 6in normal; 33ft 6in max. (*Bismarck*); 32ft normal; 37ft max. (*Tirpitz*).

Builders
Bismarck Blohm & Voss, laid down 1 July 1936; launched 14 February 1939; completed 24 August 1940.
Tirpitz Wilhelmshaven Shipyard, laid down 26 October 1936; launched 1 April 1939; completed 25 February 1941.

Armament
8×15in 47cal in twin mountings
12×5.9in 55cal in twin mountings
16×4.1in 65cal
16×37mm AA
No torpedo tubes.

Armour (Improved Krupp)
Main belt: 12¾in

Upper belt: 10¾in–5¾in
Lower belt: 6¾in
Longitudinal bulkhead: 1½in
Citadel armour: 5¾in
Barbettes: 13½in–8½in
Turrets: 14in faces, 8½in–6in sides, 12½in–7in rears, 5in roofs
Secondary turrets: 1½in
Secondary barbettes: 1½in
Anti-torpedo bulkheads: 1¾in
Conning tower: 14in
Conning tower tube: 8¾in
Upper deck: 2in

Outer deck: 3¼in, over magazines 3in, over steering gear 4¼in
Lower deck slopes: 4¼in.

Machinery
Three Blohm & Voss turbines (*Tirpitz* Brown Boveri) driving three screws, twelve Wagner boilers (oil) in three groups.

Designed SHP
138,000 for 29 knots.

Fuel
3,287 tons oil min.; 7,775 tons max.

(*Bismarck*); 2,952 tons oil min.; 8,641 tons max. (*Tirpitz*).

Radius
9,280 nm at 16 knots (*Bismarck*); 10,200 nm at 16 knots (*Tirpitz*).

Complement
2,092 (*Bismarck*); 2,340 (*Tirpitz*).

Fates
Bismarck sunk by gunfire and torpedoes 27 May 1941.
Tirpitz sunk by 5.5-ton bombs from British aircraft 12 November 1944.

40. *König*'s engine room. In general, German machinery was very reliable but not as advanced as that in the Royal Navy; the German heavy units did not change over to turbines until 1912 (*Kaiser*). The machinery/boiler installation weighed much less and took up a smaller area than in similar British units, but were considered cramped by Admiralty standards.

41. *Kronprinz*, renamed *Kronprinz Wilhelm* in December 1918. Her good underwater bulkheads and tight compartmentation stood her in good stead when she was torpedoed on 6 December 1916; although her hull was opened over a large area, she was able to proceed back to base and be repaired in just three months.

40▲ 41▼

42. *Markgraf*, shortly after anchoring at Scapa Flow in November 1918. *Markgraf* was hit five times at Jutland, but sustained only superficial damage. She was in action during North Sea sweeps and carried out bombardments in the Gulf of Riga in 1917. Apart from *Grosser Kürfurst*, they all remain on the seabed in Scapa Flow, but perhaps in the future one can be raised and preserved as a museum ship.

43. *Seydlitz*. A slightly longer and less beamier version of *Moltke*, *Seydlitz* was built as a single unit, reflecting careful design qualities. Other than the *Derfflinger* group, she was perhaps the best German battlecruiser ever built. The basic layout of *Moltke* was retained, but an extra deck level was added to the forecastle, making her a much better seaboat than the former; a feature, it may be added, which probably saved her from sinking on her way home from the Jutland action in June 1916. She was exceptionally well protected for a ship of her type, as her war experience proved. She was present at all major surface actions from 1914 to 1918: Dogger Bank, Jutland and the bombardment of Yarmouth, Hartlepool and Lowestoft. The photograph shows her damaged after the Battle of Dogger Bank in January 1915 when her after turrets were hit by heavy shells.

▲42 ▼43

Seydlitz brennend während der Seeschlacht

44, 45. *Seydlitz.* At Jutland on 31 May 1916, she was incredibly lucky to survive having been hit by 22 heavy shells and one torpedo. During the action in the 'Run to the South' she engaged the battlecruisers *Queen Mary* and *Tiger* and later fired again at *Warspite, Colossus* and *Tiger*. At the battle's end, she was a complete wreck (98 dead, 55 wounded) leaking in many places, and by 1900 hours on 1 June had 5,308 tons of water inside her hull. Miraculously, however, she entered dock on 3 June with a forward draught of 46 feet. The photographs show her conning tower from the port side with damage received during the action, and also how she lay in dock at Wilhelmshaven. Note the 11in guns have been removed to reduce top weight.

46. *Seydlitz* and *Hindenburg* on manoeuvres in 1917. With

45 ▲

repairs not completed until September and trials following, she did not join the fleet again until November 1916. She saw no more action, and spent the

rest of the war scouting or on attempted sorties. She was part of the great fleet that was sent to Scapa Flow in November 1918.

44 ▲

46 ▼

▲47 ▼48

47. *Seydlitz* in September 1917, in full fighting shape but with no one to fight. After Jutland the High Seas Fleet kept a low profile. Note the spotting tops fitted late in 1914/15.

▼49

48. *Seydlitz*, shortly after anchoring in Scapa Flow on 24 November 1918. Note that her anti-torpedo nets and booms have been removed. After being scuttled she lay keel out of the water and rested on the bottom for about nine years before attempts were made to raise her. Successful methods of salvaging were introduced and she was raised and towed away to be scrapped on 2 November 1928. Scrapping did not start immediately, but by 1930 only her hull was left.

49. *Lützow* on trials in 1915. Rather than just improve on the previous layout (*Seydlitz*), the *Lützow* group were completely redesigned which resulted in what were probably the finest battlecruisers built from 1912 to

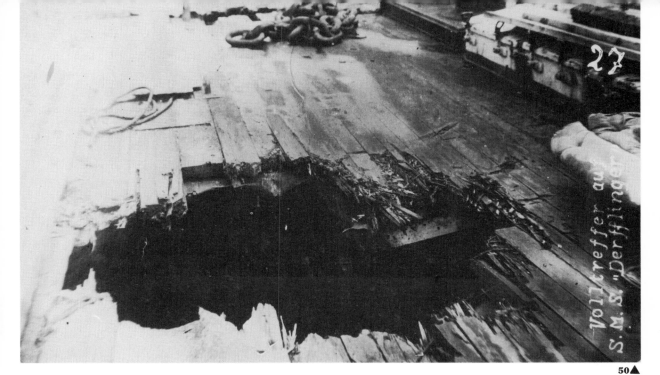

Volltreffer auf S.M.S. "Derfflinger"

50▲

1917. A classic layout of main armament (superimposed turrets forward and aft); very good armour protection – better than that of *Seydlitz* – and some oil-fired boilers introduced for propulsion, giving them a fair turn of speed (28 knots). They were handsome ships with their flush deck, rising sheer forward, and partly encased funnels.

50. *Derfflinger*, showing

damage received at Jutland. After *Seydlitz*, *Derfflinger*, was the most battle-scarred vessel to survive Jutland. She was also in all major surface actions throughout the war, proving to be a very tough opponent indeed. At Dogger Bank in January 1915 she was hit three times by heavy shells, but sustained only minimal damage. At Jutland, however, she took 21 hits from 12in, 13.5in and

15in shells, resulting in about 3,300 tons of seawater entering her hull, and killing 157 men. Her own guns hit the British *Tiger* and *Lion* at Dogger Bank and *Queen Mary*, *Tiger* and *Invincible* at Jutland.

51. *Derfflinger* at Scapa Flow in November 1918. Note the wide spread of the tripod foremast (fitted 1916), high position of the 5.9in secondary battery,

88mm guns amidships, height of armour belt (reached flush with weather deck), SL arrangement and strange funnel casing. The class could be identified by their individual funnels: *Lützow*, equal height and fully cased fore funnel; *Derfflinger*, higher fore funnel, tall uncased sections to both; *Hindenburg*, equal height funnels with short distinctive caps.

51▼

▲52 ▼53

52. *Hindenburg* at Scapa Flow in 1918. A slight improvement over *Derfflinger* was enough to place *Hindenburg* in a class of her own – much the same as *Lion* and *Queen Mary*. Most of the differences were internal, but in appearance she could always be identified from the other two. Completed in October 1917, she never saw action and so was deprived of the chance to prove herself as her half-sisters had done, but there can be no doubt that she would have been a tough opponent; she was a remarkable ship for her time.

53. *Bayern* in 1918. Britain's first look at Germany's 15in gunned ships. By 1917, after much interrogation of prisoners captured from both army and navy, sufficient information had been gathered to form the conclusion that the German Navy possessed ships armed with 15in guns. But the Admiralty had no certain information as to dimensions, displacement or numbers of ships involved. They rightfully assumed that these were probably enlarged versions of the *König* class, armed with 15in guns, but lack of detailed information was still not enough to fully appreciate the type of ship that had been built.

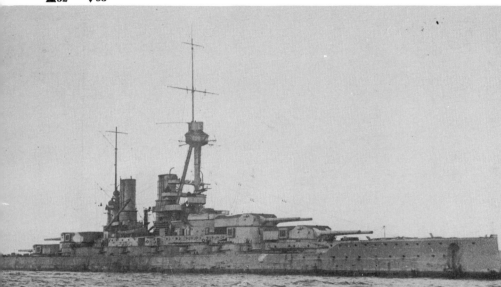

▼54

54. *Baden*, arriving at Portsmouth. Excellent ships in most repects, there was no question of their being copies of the British *Queen Elizabeth* class as was often claimed in the Press at the time. They were simply uprated versions of *König* – a powerful ship herself. *Bayern* was completed before Jutland, but was still working-up when the action took place. Both *Bayern* and *Baden* had tripod foremasts which were needed to support suitable fire control; the single familiar German pole mast had, to date,

proved inadequate for such purposes. Good-looking ships, and very hard to tell apart, the differences were evident in the bridgework, funnels and SL arrangements. They saw little war service, and were both interned at Scapa Flow in 1918. In 1919 they suffered the same fate as the rest of the German fleet when they were scuttled. *Bayern* sank, but British tugs managed to push *Baden* aground, and after being made watertight again, she was moved to Portsmouth and used for many experiments to see how

she compared with contemporary British designs.

55. On the misty morning of 21 November 1918 HMS *Cardiff* slipped quietly out of the Firth of Forth on perhaps one of the greatest naval occasions. She was to intercept the German High Seas Fleet at a pre-arranged rendezvous. The Germans were sighted at about 08.00 hours and *Cardiff* did her job by leading them back to base. They sailed between two rows of British battleships to anchor off Aberlady Bay while

the Grand Fleet anchored in the Firth. Later that day Admiral David Beatty made his famous signal: 'The German flag is to be hauled down at 15.57 today, Thursday, and is not to be hoisted again without permission.'

56. The German High Seas Fleet anchored in Scapa Flow. At dusk on 21 November the call of 'sunset' was heard, and the Imperial German flag fluttered down for the last time.

▲57

57. *Baden*'s quarterdeck. After British constructors had examined her thoroughly, she was used as a target to see how her thick armour protection would fare against British heavy shells. The conclusions were that, although an excellent ship, she was not superior to the *Royal Sovereign* to which she was compared.

▼58

▼59

58. *Bayern* sinking at Scapa Flow, 21 June 1919. Although British personnel tried to board her, she had reached danger level before anything could be done, and all the vessels that were intended to sink were lost, with the exception of *Baden*.

59. Officers in *König Albert* pose under a 12in gun turret for a photograph to send back home – not knowing when they themselves would eventually be released.

60. April 1919. Crew in *König Albert*. Demoralized, fed up, dirty and imprisoned in their ships, German crews laze about trying to keep themselves occupied.

61. Quarterdeck of *Hindenburg*, spring of 1919. The ship seems to be nice and clean unlike some of the other vessels which were left to rot by their crews. Note the turret shapes.

60 ▲   61 ▼

62. The end of *Hindenburg*. The great battlecruiser had met her end at the hands of her own crew – an inglorious fate for such a fine vessel.

63. *Deutschland* fitting out, 1932. The construction of this class arose from force of circumstances (because of naval tonnage restrictions then obtaining) rather than any planned strategic operations. To comply with a displacement limit of 10,000 tons (Treaty of Versailles) German constructors were faced with great difficulties. Nevertheless, they were able to produce a revolutionary design and arm it with six 11in guns on a speed of 26 knots. Although officially stated to be 10,000 tons, displacement was in excess by about 6,000 tons in the full load. In all essentials, the new ships were armoured cruisers of an exceptionally powerful type, but the Press incorrectly dubbed them 'pocket battleships' (the German term was *Panzerschiffe*) and in time their true worth

▲ 62

became greatly inflated. *Deutschland* was laid down in 1929 with another two ships following in 1931 and 1932. The

later two were slightly modified from *Deutschland* with regard to armouring and forward bridgework. Note the external

bulge in the hull, and the long row of scuttles which indicate an absence of armour above the main deck.

▼ 63

64 ▲

65 ▲

64. *Deutschland* in 1933. Great savings in weight were made by extensive use of electric welding in all parts of the ships, and coupled with the introduction of diesel engines for the main form of propulsion it was possible to give more weight percentage to other areas. This extra weight saved was, in the main, given to the heavy armament. The diesel engines, however, did not prove very successful, and in practice were heavier than envisaged, required more space than usual, were noisy and the vibration placed unneccessary strain on the hull seams. Construction of the ships was received with mixed feelings in Great Britain – some seeing them as a revolutionary concept, while another body of opinion saw them as 'too many eggs in one basket' and wondered what had been sacrificed to keep the displacement at about 10,000 tons.

65. *Graf Spee* as completed, 1936. Seen here fitting out before commissioning. Shortly before they were laid down, the bridgework layout was altered in the last two ships. Instead of being tubular, it became a tall, flush tower construction – indeed it was rather impressive, and gave them a much heavier appearance. As completed, and after trials, it was seen that the massive structure was a failure, and was extremely prone to catch the wind in all directions. As a result, when the opportunity came, it was altered back to that of the *Deutschland*'s fitting (*Graf Spee* was never altered, but *Scheer* received hers in 1940).

66. *Deutschland* in 1935. Although well armed, the scale of protection was not adequate for ships armed with 11in guns, which would probably engage ships with at least 8in guns. It

was stated at the time that the protective qualities were more than adequate to meet ships armed with 6in and 8in guns, but being given only 4in – 5in on the waterline, this is difficult to understand – the thickness could be pierced by 8in and badly damaged by 6in shells. All

three had good seakeeping qualities, but proved to be wet in a seaway. *Deutschland* is seen here after refit in 1935, showing modifications such as gunnery control, new SL arrangements and a fixed mast to the rear of the funnel.

66 ▼

▲67

67. *Graf Spee* in 1936, fully manned coming out of harbour. Note the crest on hull. They never really had contemporary equals, because they had been designed to outrun anything that could outshoot them, and they in turn, were supposed to be able to outshoot anything that could catch them. *Scheer* and *Graf Spee* were easy to

identify by slightly different bridgework, and mast positions.

68. *Graf Spee* in 1937–38. The pocket battleships were employed as surface raiders at the start of the war, a role in which they proved most successful. *Graf Spee* got off to a good start by sinking 50,089 tons of shipping. Her famous

action at the River Plate on 13 December 1939 brought her career to an end when she was faced with the British cruisers *Ajax*, *Achilles* and *Exeter*. All four ships were damaged, and *Graf Spee* took refuge in Montevideo. Finally, to save more bloodshed, Captain Langsdorf took *Graf Spee* out of harbour and scuttled her.

69. *Graf Spee* after blowing up, 17 December 1939. A much needed victory for the Royal Navy in the dark months of late 1939. When Winston Churchill addressed the crew of *Exeter*, after their return (15 February 1940) he said: 'In this sombre dark winter, when, apart from the Navy, we have been at war and yet not at war; in these long winter months, we have had to watch the agony of Poland and now of Finland, the brilliant action of Plate, in which you played a memorable part, came like a flash of light and colour on the scene, carrying with it an encouragement to all those who are fighting – to ourselves and to our allies; and carrying with it the cause of rejoicing to free men and to free people all over the world. You cannot but recognize that you had the fortune to be on the spot when the opportunity came. All over the world, as you know, your comrades in the Royal Navy are ardently and eagerly waiting to emulate your example.'

70. *Admiral Scheer* in 1942 (aerial view). *Scheer* entered Wilhelmshaven in February 1940 for a much needed refit, but while in dock, she was partly reconstructed. Her large flat tower forward was removed

▼69

68▲

and replaced by something similar to *Deutschland* (*Deutschland* renamed *Lützow* in November 1939), a cowl was fitted to the funnel, the bows were altered to give a more raked shape for improved seakeeping qualities, and her AA armament was increased. She left dock with a considerably different appearance. Both

Scheer and *Lützow* had extremely busy wars, and were the work-horses of the German Navy for many years. In their role of raiders, they were excellent, and both ships sank thousands of tons of enemy shipping.

71. *Scheer*: close-up of the bridge and funnel (new taller

cap), 1944. Her new mast is thicker than that of *Lützow* and had more platforms fitted to it. SL arrangements were also different and AA additions were: *Lützow* twenty-six 20mm; *Scheer* twenty-four 20mm. Both survived until almost the end of the war; *Scheer* was caught by British bombers and hit five times at Kiel on 9 April 1945.

She finally capsized in dock, and part of her is still there today, after the dock was filled in with concrete. *Lützow* settled on the bottom after near misses by 5.5-ton bombs dropped on 16 April 1945. Her guns still above water, she operated and fought on until finally blown up by her own crew on 4 May 1945.

70▼

71▼

72. *Gneisenau* in 1938; close-up, port side showing bridgework and funnel as completed. Note the thick 14in armoured belt, twin 5.9in turrets and 4.7in armament. To counter the three *Deutschland* class ships on completion, France had laid down two powerful 26,000-ton ships armed with 13in guns and capable of 31 knots – certainly more than a match for the German ships then under construction (1932–4). When Adolf Hitler came to power in 1933, however, one of his first moves was to initiate further construction to increase his maritime strength. Against the two French ships a design was drawn up that would completely outclass them and from 1934 the first layouts were being considered. At first they were nothing more than improved *Deutschland*s, but later, when more details had been worked out, it showed a powerful warship indeed. Classed as battlecruisers they had retained an 11in armament, but protection was very much on a battleship scale (14in) and speeds of 31 knots were planned. Provision for another ship (*Scharnhorst*) was made during the same year, and they became the *Scharnhorst* class. As displacement restrictions were still in force, the released figure gave 26,000 tons, but in reality they were 31,800 tons normal and 38,000 tons deep.

73. *Gneisenau* at Kiel in 1938, shortly after completion. The final design was based on that of the *Mackensen* class (1917) which had been planned at the end of the First World War, and as completed the *Scharnhorst* class heralded the return of Germany as a respectable sea power – even though small in numbers. They were first-class ships and good all-rounders – adequately armed, well armoured, good seaboats and very fast for their size. Again, as with *Deutschland*, weight was saved by extensive use of electric welding and put into extra armour and high-pressure machinery. Note the elevation (45°) of the 11in gun.

▲72   ▼73

74. *Gneisenau* in 1938, on trials. Note how the bows are smothered in water even when conditions are smooth. The straight stem was to prove inadequate, and in a seaway both vessels shipped hundreds of tons of water over the forecastle. Shortly after trials,

75. *Gneisenau* in 1938. They were often criticized for being under-gunned, but the 11in

however, *Gneisenau* was fitted with a new bow (*Scharnhorst* received hers in 1939) which, although it proved to be better, still left them wet ships forward.

54calibre piece was a first-class weapon capable of piercing all but the thickest armour. By 1941, however, plans were afoot to convert them to 15in gunned ships. After being damaged by bombs in February 1942, it was decided to fit *Gneisenau* with six 15in guns while making good

the damage. Photographs were taken by reconnaissance aircraft showing her without turrets and minus her bow (with a view to lengthening the ship).

74 ▲

75 ▼

▲76 ▼77

▼78

76, 77. *Scharnhorst* in April 1943. *Scharnhorst* met her end during the last classic sea battle of its type (no air action in the encounter). She had spent the last part of 1943 in Norwegian waters and then in December was sent to attack a British convoy off the North Cape. The mission proved unsuccessful; she never contacted the Russia-bound convoy, but did make contact with a supporting force which included the battleship *Duke of York*. The action started in the dark on 26 December 1943, when *Duke of York* opened fire at 29,700 yards by radar, and then the cruiser *Belfast* lit up the sky by starshell as ranges reduced. *Scharnhorst* put up a terrific and brave fight, but was pounded from all sides by *Duke of York*, *Belfast*, *Norfolk* and *Jamaica* as well as being attacked by destroyers. At first she was able to get away, but was slowed down when hit by torpedoes. She was hit fourteen times by 14in shells from the British battleship and by shells from the cruisers, and is stated to have been struck by about twelve torpedoes resulting in some 1,803 men killed.

78. *Bismarck* fitting out in 1940. There was no doubt whatsoever that Germany was re-arming at a rapid pace during the 1930s and had laid down two 35,000-ton battleships even after the Anglo-German Agreement of 1935 had been signed. Always stated to be 35,000-ton ships (although not fooling British Intelligence), it was not until after the war that it was realized that they were actually 41,700 tons light load, with dimensions of 794ft x 118ft. Many designs had been considered before going ahead with construction, but as completed, they were, after the Japanese *Yamato* and US *Iowa*, the largest battleships ever built.

79. *Bismarck* in 1940. Basically they were greatly developed editions of the 15in-gunned *Baden* and *Bayern*, the last German battleships completed before the end of the First World War. The huge rise in displacement from that class was due to the demand for increased protection. They were not revamped editions of 1914-18 designs but, because the *Baden* pair were such good ships, the German constructors saw no reason to change their methods and *Bismarck* and *Tirpitz* reflect many of the earlier ships' features. Outward appearance, however, bore no resemblance to earlier designs at all, in fact they were very much like the *Scharnhorst* group. When the design was studied by British Intelligence after the war, it was thought that in general it showed no advance over 1918 designs, simply because the German Navy had failed to appreciate the new conditions of warfare – plunging shellfire and bomb development. That *Bismarck* was so hard to sink seems to be attributed to her massive beam, tight compartmentation and improved armour quality.

80. *Bismarck* fitting out, 1940. The armour used for *Bismarck* and *Tirpitz* was an improved version of the Krupps process called 'Woten hard' and 'Woten soft' and had a much greater resistance to shellfire. In appearance the ships resembled *Scharnhorst*, with their single funnel and distribution of superstructure forward and aft, but with an extra turret worked in and twin instead of triple mountings. *Bismarck* was a balanced design and proved to be a good seaboat with an exceptionally fast speed for a ship of such a size. The *Bismarck* episode is probably the most famous naval action of the Second World War. With convoy destruction their intention, *Bismarck* and the heavy cruiser *Prinz Eugen* had set out on 18 May 1941, and anchored off Bergen to refuel on 21 May. While at anchor, she was spotted by reconnaissance aircraft and the Admiralty was alerted. On 22 May both ships set course for the Denmark Strait. When about 75 miles north of Iceland, they were spotted by the British cruiser *Suffolk* which was fired on and later lost contact. Two days later, known to be in the area,

Bismarck was spotted by the battlecruiser *Hood* and battleship *Prince of Wales*. Action commenced with disastrous results for *Hood*, while *Prince of Wales* was mauled. *Bismarck* was hit three times; one of these hits was to

be the ship's undoing because it punctured the forward fuel tank and she was leaving a trail of oil behind. Down by the bows, and trying to make home base, she was torpedoed by aircraft from *Ark Royal* to slow her down, and was badly hit in the rudder,

which forced her to turn in a huge circle. On 27 May she was finally cornered by the battleships *King George V* and *Rodney*.

79▲

80▼

▲81 ▼82

▼83

81. *Bismarck* off Bergen, 21 May 1941. The cruisers *Suffolk* and *Norfolk* which had followed *Bismarck* throughout, were also in at the end. *King George V* and *Rodney* opened fire at 08.47 hours. *Bismarck* returned fire shortly afterwards. *Bismarck* was soon hit, most disastrously in the command tower which knocked out the central control for her big guns. With the cruisers' 8in guns opening up as well, *Bismarck* soon became a blazing wreck and the order was given to abandon ship. The cruiser *Dorsetshire* was sent in to finish her off with three torpedoes. *Bismarck* sank at 10.27 hours leaving only 110–115 survivors.

82. *Tirpitz* from the quarterdeck, well camouflaged from prying aircraft. After *Bismarck* was lost, *Tirpitz* was the most powerful unit in the German Navy. She spent most of 1941 fitting out and running sets of trials in home waters. In early 1942 she was based at Trondheim, and from then on remained in Norwegian waters until the end. Although Adolf Hitler had lost faith in the capital ship, the period of *Tirpitz*'s lying idle still posed a serious threat to convoys, which compelled the Royal Navy to keep big ships instantly available in case *Tirpitz* broke out to attack.

83. *Tirpitz* in 1942. Note the strange camouflage. On 22 September 1943 she was badly damaged by miniature submarines (X6 and X7); on 3 April 1944 she was seriously damaged by bombs from British aircraft (14 hits) and on 17 July 1944 and 22 August 1944 there were further attacks.

84. *Tirpitz* in 1943. Note the camouflage has been slightly altered. It was decided to try a different method of attack which would not just damage *Tirpitz* but sink her. On 15 September 1944 she was attacked by British heavy bombers with 12,000lb bombs, one of which just missed the bows but seriously damaged her and made her unseaworthy. She was later moved to Tromsö but was photographed by Intelligence on 14 October and another attack was prepared.

85. *Tirpitz*. After an unsuccessful attack on 29 October 1944, she was attacked again on 12 November 1944 by British bombers using 5.5-ton bombs. With three direct hits and several near misses she capsized in shallow water, showing about 700 feet of her keel above water once the smoke had cleared. A sad end for such a fine ship, but a neccessary one. The wreck was broken up in situ from 1948.

The *Fotofax* series

A new range of pictorial studies of military subjects for the modeller, historian and enthusiast. Each title features a carefully-selected set of photographs plus a data section of facts and figures on the topic covered. With line drawings and detailed captioning, every volume represents a succinct and valuable study of the subject. New and forthcoming titles:

Warbirds
F-111 Aardvark
P-47 Thunderbolt
B-52 Stratofortress
Stuka!
Jaguar
US Strategic Air Power:
  Europe 1942–1945
Dornier Bombers
RAF in Germany

Vintage Aircraft
German Naval Air Service
Sopwith Camel
Fleet Air Arm, 1920–1939
German Bombers of WWI

Soldiers
World War One: 1914
World War One: 1915
World War One: 1916
Union Forces of the American
  Civil War
Confederate Forces of the
  American Civil War
Luftwaffe Uniforms
British Battledress 1945–1967
  (2 vols)

Warships
Japanese Battleships, 1897–
  1945
Escort Carriers of World War
  Two
German Battleships, 1897–
  1945
Soviet Navy at War, 1941–1945
US Navy in World War Two,
  1943–1944
US Navy, 1946–1980 (2 vols)
British Submarines of World
  War One

Military Vehicles
The Chieftain Tank
Soviet Mechanized Firepower
  Today
British Armoured Cars since
  1945
NATO Armoured Fighting
  Vehicles
The Road to Berlin
NATO Support Vehicles

The *Illustrated* series

The internationally successful range of photo albums devoted to current, recent and historic topics, compiled by leading authors and representing the best means of obtaining your own photo archive.

Warbirds
US Spyplanes
USAF Today
Strategic Bombers, 1945–1985
Air War over Germany
Mirage
US Naval and Marine Aircraft
  Today
USAAF in World War Two
B-17 Flying Fortress
Tornado
Junkers Bombers of World War
  Two
Argentine Air Forces in the
  Falklands Conflict
F-4 Phantom Vol II
Army Gunships in Vietnam
Soviet Air Power Today
F-105 Thunderchief
Fifty Classic Warbirds
Canberra and B-57
German Jets of World War Two

Vintage Warbirds
The Royal Flying Corps in
  World War One
German Army Air Service in
  World War One
RAF between the Wars
The Bristol Fighter
Fokker Fighters of World War
  One
Air War over Britain, 1914–
  1918
Nieuport Aircraft of World War
  One

Tanks
Israeli Tanks and Combat
  Vehicles
Operation Barbarossa
Afrika Korps
Self-Propelled Howitzers
British Army Combat Vehicles
  1945 to the Present
The Churchill Tank
US Mechanized Firepower
  Today
Hitler's Panzers
Panzer Armee Afrika
US Marine Tanks in World War
  Two

Warships
The Royal Navy in 1980s
The US Navy Today
NATO Navies of the 1980s
British Destroyers in World
  War Two
Nuclear Powered Submarines
Soviet Navy Today
British Destroyers in World
  War One
The World's Aircraft Carriers,
  1914–1945
The Russian Convoys, 1941–
  1945
The US Navy in World War
  Two
British Submarines in World
  War Two
British Cruisers in World War
  One
U-Boats of World War Two
Malta Convoys, 1940–1943

Uniforms
US Special Forces of World
  War Two
US Special Forces 1945 to the
  Present
The British Army in Northern
  Ireland
Israeli Defence Forces, 1948 to
  the Present
British Special Forces, 1945 to
  Present
US Army Uniforms Europe,
  1944–1945
The French Foreign Legion
Modern American Soldier
Israeli Elite Units
US Airborne Forces of World
  War Two
The Boer War
The Commandos World War
  Two to the Present
Victorian Colonial Wars

UNION FORCES OF THE AMERICAN CIVIL WAR — Soldiers Fotofax

P-47 THUNDERBOLT — Warbirds Fotofax

WORLD WAR ONE: 1914 — Soldiers Fotofax

THE CHIEFTAIN TANK — Military Vehicles Fotofax

F-111 AARDVARK — Warbirds Fotofax

ESCORT CARRIERS OF WORLD WAR TWO — Warships Fotofax

JAPANESE BATTLESHIPS 1897–1945 — Warships Fotofax

GERMAN NAVAL AIR SERVICE — Vintage Aviation Fotofax

A catalogue listing these series and other Arms & Armour Press titles is available on request from: Sales Department, Arms & Armour Press, Artillery House, Artillery Row, London SW1P 1RT.